THE GHOSTLY TALES OF CENTRAL NEW MEXICO

Published by Arcadia Children's Books
A Division of Arcadia Publishing, Inc.
Charleston, SC
www.arcadiapublishing.com

First published 2026
Manufactured in the United States

Designed by Jessica Nevins
Images used courtesy of Shutterstock.com.

ISBN: 9781467196178
Library of Congress Control Number: 2025948425

Spooky America

The Ghostly Tales of Central New Mexico

Lisha Cauthen

Adapted from *Ghost Stories of Central New Mexico* by Cody Polston

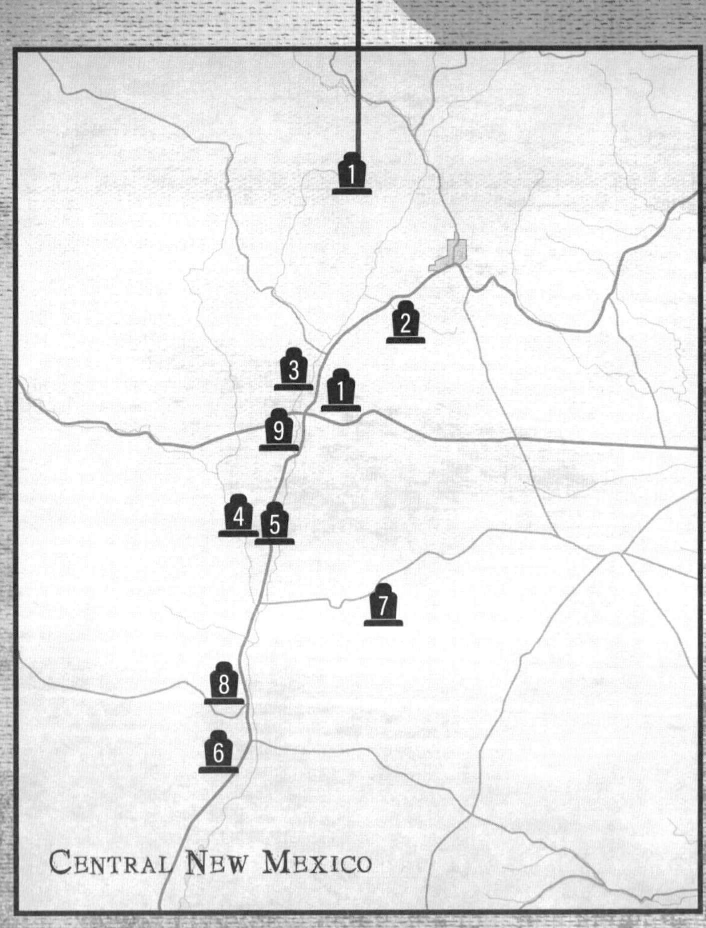
Colorado
Kansas
Oklah
New Mexico
Arizona
Texas
1
2
3
1
9
4
5
7
8
6
Central New Mexico

Table of Contents & Map Key

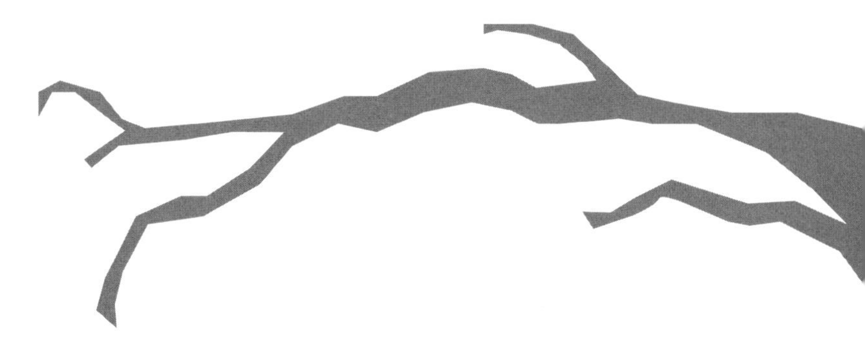

Welcome to Spooky Central New Mexico!

Imagine it is a June day in 1706, and you are standing inside an adobe church with five-foot-thick walls. Adobe bricks are made from air-dried mud, which insulates the building. Inside the church it is dark and cool and smells of incense. You'd never know that outside, the heat is suffocating.

Your baby brother squirms in his baptismal gown. It's made from a simple cotton fabric, but your mother has painstakingly embroidered the gown with doves, flowers, and a lion lying down with a lamb. This is an important day for your family, but it's also important for the whole community of Villa San Francisco de Alburquerque. It is the first baptism held in this newly founded church in this newly named town.

Your family came from New Spain, a territory ruled by the Spanish Empire from the 1500s to 1800s that stretched from modern-day Mexico to the U.S. Southwest, and also included Central America, the Caribbean, and the Philippines. After a long, hot journey, they settled on a land grant located on the western side of the Rio Bravo. You walked for hours to get to church today, taking off your shoes and socks to wade across the river at the Atrisco Forde, where the water is usually shallow. Finally, you are all gathered in this welcoming church, out of the blazing sun.

You, your parents, and your baby brother are not the first settlers along this stretch of the Rio Bravo. Of course, the first people to call this area home were the Tewa-speaking Pueblo people. In 1598, Don Juan de Oñate claimed the region for Spain and brought families to settle this wild land. Much of the area is desert, but the Rio Bravo supplies abundant water for farming and ranching. The Spanish communities have built arroyos, which are ditches used for irrigation.

In 1680, the Spanish settlers were driven out by the Pueblo Revolt, when the Native people rose up against the Spanish government. The Spanish had outlawed the Pueblo people's religion, and the people were angry. They ran the Spanish military, governmental officials, merchants, and settlers out of the territory.

Twelve years later, the Spanish made peace with the Pueblo people, and the settlers returned. When you were a toddler, your parents arrived at the Rio Bravo and built your estancia, which is a ranch.

Now, the priest pours cold water over your baby brother's head. Your brother cries, but your mother smiles and says, "It's a lucky sign. El diablo is leaving him." Maybe so, but you aren't sure about that. You think the priest might have pinched him.

On this happy day in 1706, you have no way of knowing that an exciting future is coming. That all of New Spain will become the new nation of Mexico after the people win their battle for independence in 1821. That the Santa Fe Trail will open and bring trade with the United States. Eventually, tensions will rise between the two nations, and Mexico will lose its land east of the Rio Bravo in the Mexican-American War, fought from 1846 to 1848.

And that is just the beginning. The Rio Bravo will be called the Rio Grande in the United States.

New Mexico will be welcomed into the United States, first as a territory in 1850 and then as a state in 1912. And more than three hundred years after your baby brother's baptism, the tiny settlement of Villa San Francisco de Alburquerque will grow into the modern big city of Albuquerque.

Return to today, nearly five hundred years after the first Spaniard entered Central New Mexico. Now, the area is the home of Kirtland Air Force Base; Sandia National Lab; the longest tram in North America, Sandia Peak Tramway; and the largest hot air balloon fest in the world, the Albuquerque International Balloon Fiesta.

Ranchers, farmers, scientists, artists, business leaders, and military personnel call Central New Mexico home—but not all of the residents are among the living. If you have the nerve, turn the page and learn about the spooks and spirits that haunt this harsh but beautiful land.

And just couldn't leave . . .

Ghostly Guardians of Treasure

Central New Mexico has many tales of lost treasure. In 1540, the first European to explore the area, Francisco Vásquez de Coronado, came looking for the Seven Cities of Gold, also known as Cibola. He believed the rumors he heard—that north of the region that became Mexico, seven cities bursting with gold and other riches were there for the taking. For two years, he and his men wandered through the area that is now

Central New Mexico and then east to Kansas. But adobe pueblos and the thatched huts of Native Americans were all he found.

Did Cibola ever exist? Today, New Mexico is a hub of mining for turquoise and coal but also for gold, silver, and copper. It isn't far-fetched to believe that the ancient people of the area also mined these precious metals. Could secret cities of gold and other hidden fortunes still be waiting to be discovered?

Old prospectors often swapped stories about untold riches buried in the New Mexico wilderness. One of those tales took place during the Pueblo Revolt of 1680. A Spanish settler, Ramon Vigil, tried to flee, but his gold and silver bars, jewelry, and candlesticks were too heavy and awkward for him to carry. So, somewhere on the northern edge of the Sandia Mountains, he hid his treasure, said to be worth $250,000. (That would be more than $8.5 million today!) Soon after, some men caught Vigil. They demanded to know where he had hidden his fortune, but he refused to tell them. He died with his secret.

Later, one of these men was traveling in the Sandia Mountains by himself when he was surprised by a fierce storm. He crouched under some boulders and drew his blanket over his head to wait it out. His skin stung as the wind whipped him with frigid rain, but finally, the storm passed. He was relieved that his ordeal was over—

—except it wasn't. It had only just begun.

By now it was dark, and as the man's eyes adjusted in the moonlight, his saw an eerie figure. His flesh crawled as he realized it was the ghost of Ramon Vigil, as real and as solid as he had been in life.

The man's teeth chattered with fear. He knew that Vigil was no longer among the living. He was being haunted by a dead man!

The uncanny apparition didn't speak a word. He simply gestured for the man to follow him, and together, they climbed to the top of the mountain. There, the ghost pointed to a cave hidden by tree branches and shrubs. The man swallowed his dread and entered.

Inside, he walked and walked down a miles-long tunnel that led to an enormous cavern. The man turned to ask what the spirit wanted from him. But the ghost of Ramon Vigil had vanished.

The cavern was pitch black. The man was lost inside a mountain and utterly alone. He reached into his pouch and scraped together enough kindling to light a small flame. Then his jaw dropped.

Because spread before him was Ramon Vigil's treasure. But that was not all. The walls of the cave were so packed with gold, the gleam from it dazzled him, even in his feeble firelight. The cave was also piled with boulders of gold that were so big, a dozen men could not lift even one of them. For hours, he wandered the cavern, stunned by the sparkling riches. Finally, he found a flight of stairs made entirely of gold that led outside.

He climbed out of the cavern and shook his head in amazement. Why would Vigil's spirit show him where the treasure was? Why would he tell a secret after his death that he wouldn't reveal when he was alive?

It didn't matter. All that mattered was that he, alone, knew the location of Vigil's treasure. Carefully, he marked the cave entrance so that he could find it again. Then, under the cold moonlight, he hurried to fetch help to retrieve the riches.

The next day, he brought dozens of men to carry out the precious things. It would take many trips to bring all those valuables back to their homes. Confidently, he led the men up the mountain and looked for the markings he'd left at the cave, but he couldn't find them.

Maybe he was mistaken. It was easy to get confused in these mountains. He climbed a little farther.

Still no cave. He searched east, then west, growing more and more frantic. Where was the cave? Where was the treasure? Hour after hour, he and the men searched. But it was no use. The treasure's resting place was again a mystery.

If you decide to hunt for Ramon Vigil's treasure in the Sandia Mountains, watch out, especially if you are caught in a sudden storm. It just may be the ghost of Ramon Vigil, coming to trick you too.

In the 1800s, prospectors and commercial operators mined all around the Central New Mexico area. Towns would appear seemingly overnight as mining operations opened, and when they closed, the towns would disappear just as quickly. But one town disappeared more quickly than most.

In the Jemez Mountains near New Mexico Highway 44, the locals often report seeing strange lights in the distance after dark. One terrifying night, a cowboy found out exactly where those lights come from.

The cowboy was riding toward an estancia where he often worked mending fences and rounding up cattle. The night was quiet, and he was enjoying the sweet smell of sage as his horse brushed past the bushes. When he came over a rise, he saw lights that looked like a good-sized town in the valley below him.

The cowboy was puzzled. He had lived here all his life and knew the area well. There was no town in this valley, only wide-open space. He rode down the gully to find out what was going on.

He soon found himself in a sizeable town, with lights glowing inside each of the buildings. But absolutely no one was on the street. Curious, he rode up to one of the houses, jumped off his horse, and knocked on the door.

Fwoof!

The lights all over town suddenly blew out. Spooked, the cowboy jumped on his horse and galloped away.

When the cowboy got to the estancia, his companions could see he was shaken. So, the next morning, he and a friend rode back to find the mysterious town.

But the town was gone. No homes. No saloon. No church. Nothing was there, except a single, crumbling adobe foundation.

Today, the locals know better than to be lured away by the mysterious lights. If you decide to investigate, be prepared. You may be entering a ghost town that is *truly* full of ghosts.

Many people have mined the riches of the land here, and they often find it hard to leave, even in death. One old prospector thought his cabin near the mining community of Elizabethtown was so cozy, his spirit is probably still there.

In 1899, Harry Lyons had been dead for two years. But he was still causing his neighbor, Mr. Wilson, so much trouble that Wilson complained about it to the *Las Vegas Optic* newspaper. Wilson said that he was continually closing the doors and windows to the Lyons cabin, only to find them open again each time he returned. Things inside the house were moved around, and sometimes, the hair on the back of Wilson's neck would prickle as he heard Lyons whistling, talking, and laughing.

The newspaper article ends:

"He says that heretofore he has not been a believer in spirits of any kind, either fermented or those of the departed, but he does believe there is something of that kind around the Lyon cabin now."

Do a tricky apparition, a phantom town, and a whistling spirit tickle your ghost-hunting curiosity? If so, turn the page . . .

The Coal-mining Spirits of Madrid

Follow the Turquoise Trail up New Mexico Highway 14 to Madrid, a coal-mining community that was deserted and left a ghost town for thirty years. Though Madrid is now a vibrant arts community, don't let the bright jewelry shops, intriguing art galleries, and crowded restaurants fool you. The ghosts have never really left.

Madrid is located in New Mexico's Coal

Gulch area in the Ortiz Mountains and was once a coal-mining company town with a population of 2,500. But one morning in December 1932, an explosion rocked the mine.

Friends and family heard the explosion and rushed from their homes, anxious for their loved ones' safety. Hundreds waited all day in the cold, shivering around small fires, as rescuers frantically searched for the miners. The people in the crowd waited for word on their husbands, fathers, and sons.

It took all day, but finally, the bodies

of fourteen miners were recovered. Six miners were injured, and thirty-three miners emerged shaken but unhurt. The bodies of the victims were loaded into open trucks and transported to the local hospital morgue a mile away in Madrid. The solemn spectators followed on foot.

The mine and the town recovered for a while, but the coal industry faded, and the mine closed in the 1950s. Before long, residents fled Madrid, leaving the abandoned town to its ghosts.

In the 1970s, people began moving back, but the spirits never left. When you visit, will you see the ghostly mourners from the mining explosion of 1932 following the phantom trucks carrying their deceased loved ones? Or hear the *clink-clink-clink* of miners still hard at work?

Perhaps. But your best chance of experiencing something out of the ordinary might be a visit to the local restaurant and bar, the Mine Shaft Tavern. When the tavern opened in 1947, it had the longest stand-up bar in New Mexico. It seems miners enjoyed having a relaxing drink while standing up straight, after they had spent a difficult shift bent over in the mine.

Your first clue that something strange is going on at the Mine Shaft Tavern might come when you see glasses fly off the bar and explode into pieces. Your next clue might be when the bar doors begin to swing back and forth, though no one is anywhere near them. Could it be long-dead miners, blowing off steam after a hard day underground?

Employees will tell you they often feel spooked after hours, when they close up for the night. Sometimes, the hair on their arms stands up. Glasses, plates, and utensils end up in strange places all on their own. Chilling noises echo in the walls.

But chills, weird noises, and shattering glass are the *least* of the tavern's paranormal troubles. Staff and visitors have documented many apparitions throughout the building. For instance, they often spot the shadow of a woman wearing a long dress near the stage area. Could it be the wife of a dead miner, looking for her husband? Or is it a waitress from times gone by, still delivering drinks from the bar?

The most commonly encountered ghost hangs out near the restrooms. The "restroom ghost" is a real troublemaker. She pokes people in the backside as they walk down the corridor, and once in a while, she wraps her spectral hands around women's necks and tries to strangle them. Some unnerved tavern-goers have reported seeing the spirit materialize in a bathroom stall, emerge, and then vanish. If you decide to visit the bathroom, don't look in a mirror, or you may see the restroom ghost's ghastly reflection looking back at you.

Sometimes, the restroom ghost raids the kitchen to smash dishes on the floor, and other times she's in the bar, violently flicking the lights on and off.

Who is this troublesome ghost? Experts believe it is the spirit of a young lady who died in a car accident directly outside the tavern. And by all reports, she is angry about it.

People who want to work at the tavern have to be prepared for anything. One former bartender said that sometimes, while closing up at 3:00 a.m., he'd see movement out of the corner of his eye. He'd turn off a light, only to have it flicker and flash blindingly bright before it finally went dark. Shadows crept across the walls, even after the lights were out.

Once, he approached a couple at the end of the bar to refresh their drinks but then hesitated. A strange cloud of smoke hovered over the couple—even though no one in the room was smoking. The bartender watched the cloud, mesmerized, as the smoke simply disappeared. Was it the spirit of a miner, looking for one last drink?

Another employee has witnessed so much weird phenomena, she has no choice but to believe in the supernatural. One night, she was walking through the mine tunnel that leads to the stage area when she saw the silhouette of a man. He looked like a cowboy, leaning against the mine shaft wall with his boot up and his head down. As she started to speak to him, he suddenly disappeared.

The employee agrees that at the Mine Shaft

Tavern, it's not unusual for drinks to move around on the bar on their own or shadowy figures to appear out of nowhere. The employee says, "People ask if this place is haunted. And while it may be easier to say no, the answer is very much yes."

It may surprise you to find out you don't have to go inside the tavern to encounter a haunting. One man told about an eerie experience he had just walking by the tavern building on a bright, sunny day. As he passed the establishment, the front door creaked open, slowly, as wide as it

possibly could. Then, it swung closed, inch by inch, until finally—*BAM!*—it slammed shut.

The man ran back to his car as fast as he could.

Many people would, but maybe your nerves are made of steel. If so, turn the page to find out about a house full of history—and ghosts.

The Old Haunted House of Corrales

Travel north of Albuquerque and up the Rio Grande to the town of Corrales, where you'll find a place jam-packed with history—and hauntings.

Pueblo people settled here before 500 CE. Then, in the 1500s, Spanish settlers moved in, and in the early 1700s, the Martinez family built a home here. Over the following 300 years, the structure served as a home, courthouse, cavalry headquarters, convent, stagecoach stop, mental hospital, tuberculosis sanatorium, and grocery store. Today, the building is a restaurant called Casa Vieja, which means "old house."

Step into Casa Vieja and you will find fourteen rooms with thirty-inch-thick adobe walls, hand-carved doors, seven working fireplaces, and enormous vigas, or large wooden beams that support the roof. For many years, the Corrales area was a hostile territory, so gun turrets for defense were once installed along the walls.

The building holds many secrets. In the old days, it was common to stash valuables within the thick adobe walls to conceal them from attackers. Many hidden items have been uncovered during the multiple renovations on the building. Coins, weird statues, and a 16th century Spanish sword have all been discovered. A portrait of Duke Nogaret de La Valette that was painted in the 1600s has been recovered; you can see it hanging in the restaurant today.

But not all of the nooks and crannies have been explored. Rumors abound that an ivory-and-gold statue of Our Lady of Guadalupe is still concealed somewhere inside the restaurant. Curious visitors have been known to pound on the walls, trying to determine whether they are hollow or if a treasure is inside, still waiting to be revealed. Maybe you'll try your luck with a well-placed thump or two.

The first public story about the strange goings-on at Casa Vieja appeared in the *Albuquerque Journal* newspaper in 1987. The Bentley family had restored the old building and opened it as a restaurant. And then eerie things began to happen.

The elegant restaurant featured lit candles on every table. Often, when it was time to close, an unseen helper didn't want the fun to end.

As servers went from table to table, blowing out the candles, the spirit would follow behind and relight them. One waiter had so many odd experiences with the ghost, he felt he knew its name: Harold.

It's hard to figure out exactly who Harold is—a Spanish soldier, a stagecoach driver, or a member of the Martinez family? After all, thousands of people have lived in, worked at, and visited Casa Vieja over the past 300 years.

Jim White took over the restaurant in 1999. At first, he didn't believe in ghosts, but he soon changed his mind. First it was small things, like lights flickering and glasses and pitchers crashing to the floor for no reason. Then dinner plates placed before diners began to move and glasses floated in the air, lifted by invisible hands.

And for a long while, every night, White and his wife would close the restaurant, carefully lock every door, and set the burglar alarm. In the morning, they would find all the doors wide open, though the alarm never sounded. No one could possibly have entered the building without setting off the security system.

No one alive, that is.

Jim White and the staff weren't the only ones to have ghostly encounters at Casa Vieja. Guests have had spooky experiences too. One couple arrived at the restaurant to have dinner with friends who were already seated. As the couple made their way across the room to their friends' table, they saw a dense cloud of smoke hanging over it, which slowly dissipated as they got closer. No one in the room was smoking a cigarette, so where did the cloud come from? And where did it go? Was it a friendly phantom who just wanted to get in on the conversation?

In 2016, Linda and Gary Socha bought Casa

Vieja. Owning a haunted restaurant sounded fun, but they were a bit skeptical. After all, it's easy to let your imagination run away with you in such an ancient place with so much history. The Sochas wondered—could the restaurant really be infested with ghosts?

They soon found out.

One day, Linda was putting away Christmas decorations when she heard a hubbub going on at the back door. She was sure she'd heard her husband, Gary, open and close the back door and stomp through the kitchen, rattling bags and making a commotion.

Only it wasn't Gary. To her horror, when Linda investigated, she found an empty kitchen. She trembled as she realized that she was the only living person in the building. Who—or what—was keeping her company?

It turns out that Linda wasn't afraid for long. Quickly, the ghost proved to be friendly, though playful, and very busy. Today, the spirit is still particularly fond of opening and closing doors. Witnesses report that heavy doors, the patio door, and even a spring-loaded door have all opened on their own.

One day, an electrician was installing a new outlet in a closet. All was going well, and Linda was working in the next room when she heard screaming, thumping, and banging. She rushed toward the ruckus to find that the electrician was trapped in the closet. It seems that the mischievous spirit had closed the door and flipped the latch to lock the electrician in!

No word on whether the electrician finished the job.

Gary took a bit longer to convince that the haunting was real. Then one day he was up a ladder in a hallway. As he worked, the bathroom door behind him slowly opened, all on its own. Gary thought it may have been an air current, so he experimented with the windows and air ducts to see if he could make the bathroom door open again. But he couldn't. "You know," he told his wife, "maybe there's something to this ghost thing."

If you have the nerve, check out the lounge where numerous witnesses report seeing a Hispanic woman dressed in white sitting near the fireplace. You might mistake her for a living, breathing woman who is enjoying the good cheer of the restaurant, until she vanishes, right before your eyes.

Then peek in the bar. Do you see a lone man, quietly sipping a drink? That might be another shy spirit that many customers have described. If you blink and he disappears, you'll know that you've seen one of the resident ghosts too.

Maybe you'll run into the specter of a Corrales politician who is said to keep an eye on the place to make sure the restaurant is successful. And if you're very lucky, you may glimpse the phantom seven-foot-tall soldier who was once the head of security when the building was a cavalry outpost. Witnesses report seeing his huge, buckled boot step through a doorway, but when they investigate, no one is there.

If you're up for it, travel south along the Rio Grande to Los Lunas to visit another restaurant, where even the ghosts have been haunted by ghosts.

The Gracious Ghost of Luna Mansion

Thirty minutes south of Albuquerque you'll find the village of Los Lunas, population 20,000 and growing. Los Lunas was a prominent crossroads on the Camino Real de Tierra Adentro, which means "Royal Road of the Interior Land." Because of that, it has been an important center for business and commerce from the very earliest days of the Spanish Colonial period. Four Caminos Reales led from Mexico City to the far corners of New Spain. The Camino Real de Tierra Adentro was built in 1598 and spanned 1,500 miles from Mexico City to Ohkay Owingeh Pueblo, just north of Santa Fe.

The Luna and Otero families founded their estancias in the Los Lunas area after their arrival in 1692. Eventually, the families intermarried. They bought and sold land, ranched, and farmed.

Generations later, in the 1880s, the Santa Fe Railroad wanted to lay track through the Luna family holdings. The Lunas agreed to grant access if the railroad built the family a magnificent mansion. It took three years and

cost $47,000 ($14,812,600 today!) to build the two-story, Southern plantation-style home. Today, the home is a beautifully maintained restaurant. And it is very haunted.

When you park in front of Luna Mansion, you may notice someone standing in a second-floor window, looking back at you. It could be an employee, getting ready for the evening rush. But don't be surprised if you find out it is the ghost of Josefita "Pepe" Otera, who died in 1951.

As you enter, take note of the picture of Salomon Luna posing with President Taft because the picture has been known to float away from the wall and then back again, as if lifted by invisible hands.

Once you've settled at your table, be prepared for your glass to suddenly tip over all by itself. And try not to shiver if you feel a sudden, phantom touch on the back of your head.

One family had an unbelievable evening at the mansion in 1987. The group was seated at a table near the entrance and appeared to be enjoying some appetizers and good conversation. So, David Scoville, the manager, was surprised when an employee asked him to stop by their table. Did they have a complaint?

When Scoville approached the group, he noticed they were sitting completely still, not talking or eating. In a shaky voice, one of the diners explained that he had just felt unseen hands tug on his ponytail! Not only had the man felt the tug, the others at the table saw his hair rise into the air on its own, though absolutely no one was near him.

After the man finished his story—*POP!*—the lightbulbs in the chandelier above the family suddenly exploded, as if the ghost wanted to have the last word. Glass shards showered them all, powdering their hair, their clothes, and their food.

From that time on, misbehaving lightbulbs have become a recurring problem for Luna Mansion. Some nights, the bulbs simply unscrew themselves, and the employees have to go from lamp to lamp, tightening them in their sockets. The spirits are particularly fond of the chandelier bulbs, and employees keep a ladder close at hand so they can keep the lights burning. If you see an unlit lamp, it might be a burned-out lightbulb. Or it may be the handiwork of a resident ghost.

“I have had six or seven real clear sightings of ghosts over the years,” says Scoville.

Watch carefully, and you too might see the ghost of a man wearing a flat-brimmed farmer’s hat. Or a woman in a blue dress who haunts the dining area. She’s often spotted walking from the kitchen to the staircase and through the dining room, where she disappears. Both of the specters are believed to be servants of the home who are still going about their duties.

One waitress claimed to hear chatty ghosts on the second floor of the mansion. "I hear conversations upstairs when no one is there," she said, "but just as soon as I realize there's talking, it stops."

The spirited incidents are almost too numerous to mention: lights flickering, an apparition in a storeroom mirror, and a locked and bolted wine cellar door that springs open and sets off the alarm though no one is there. One staff member saw a spirit appear out of one wall and disappear into another. It seems a whole host of unseen residents want to make sure that the employees and guests know they are still around.

But it's the ghost of Josefita "Pepe" Otero that you are most likely to see there. She inherited the mansion during the 1920s, and her paintings still grace the walls of the building.

Family lore says that Pepe, herself, was the first to encounter ghosts in the home. One morning she was upstairs in her bedroom when she heard voices downstairs. At the foot of the stairs, she saw a man and a woman who she thought were her servants. She called down for them to bring her some coffee.

When the coffee didn't appear, she called downstairs again. Then again. Angry that her servants had ignored her, Pepe rushed down the stairs to scold them.

But to her surprise, the house was empty, and the doors were locked. When she checked her servants' living quarters, she found that the man was bedridden with the flu and the woman had left a note—she had gone back to her home village to care for a sick relative.

Then who had she seen talking at the foot of the stairs? Pepe believed they were the ghosts of servants who had served previous family members. So, it is interesting that Pepe has become a ghost herself.

The first time Scoville saw Pepe, it was late at night, and he was alone in the building. He was upstairs in the Spirit Lounge closing up, and out of the corner of his eye, he noticed a lampshade swaying. As he turned to look, the dim image of Pepe appeared. She wore a dress from the 1920s, and her hair was pinned up in a neat bun. As he watched, she became as solid as a living human.

Terrified, Scoville forgot to close out the registers, stock up the drinks, or draw the curtains. He raced down the stairs and out the front door without looking back. When he got to the gate, he stood, panting, his heart pounding.

He turned to look up at the second-floor and saw Pepe still there. Standing at the window. Looking down at Scoville.

Once the family bedrooms, the lounge is probably your best bet for having a ghostly experience. When you visit, you may feel goosebumps, chills, or a sense of breathlessness. Some witnesses report seeing Pepe as a little old lady in a long black dress who appears for an instant and then is gone. Or Pepe may appear as she did in her youth, dressed in white.

Pepe is also said to greet visitors from her rocking chair, which is set at the top of the stairs. You can be sure that Pepe sits there frequently because there's never any dust on the armrests or seat.

If you do spot Pepe, don't be afraid. Devyn

Scoville wasn't. When she was three years old, she was watching cartoons on a television upstairs while her father worked downstairs. A lady she didn't know was keeping her company. Eventually, the lady tired of the cartoons and asked whether she could read a book to Devyn.

So, Devyn went downstairs and asked her dad for a book; she told him Josefita wanted to read to her. Startled, Scoville ran upstairs to confront the stranger in the building—but no one was there.

Today, Scoville is sure it was the ghost of Josefita "Pepe" Otero: "I had told Devyn about Josefita, but I never taught her that name. I taught her Pepe," he said. "There was no way she should have known the name Josefita back then, but that's who she said wanted to read to her."

But Pepe is not the only ghost in the village who is interested in reading. Turn the page to find out about the spirits that haunt the Los Lunas Public Library and other places . . .

Otherworldly Readers and Rail Riders

Continue your ghost hunt by walking a half-mile down Main Street to the Village of Los Lunas Public Library. Many people have encountered apparitions and other phenomena here, including Cynthia Shetter, the director of the library.

Her strange experiences began one summer day many years ago. Shetter was attending to library business when an interesting patron came in the front door. "One day, this Native American man came in and was wearing a duster [an ankle-length coat] with tall boots," she said. "He looked like he came straight out of a history book."

The visitor had a friend with him. Curious about the unusual pair, Shetter watched the man in the duster leaf through some reference books. When he was finished, he and his friend walked into the next room. Shetter followed them.

But when she got to the next room, they were nowhere to be found. She rubbed her eyes—they couldn't have just vanished into thin air . . .

. . . or could they?

She asked all the staff members working that day if they had seen where the unusual guests went, but everyone answered that they had not seen the Native American man and his friend in the first place.

Shetter had more pressing things to attend to, so she shrugged and let the mystery go. Until weeks later, when another library worker told Shetter that she had begun to see the pair repeatedly, and just as mysteriously, they would disappear.

These eerie reports intrigued paranormal researchers, who set up an investigation to try to capture evidence of ghostly activity. They were not disappointed.

They photographed orbs everywhere in the library. Orbs are balls of light that some think may be wandering spirits. Though some orbs may simply be dust or insects, the investigators found that several impressive orbs were photographed following Shetter throughout the library.

It seems the library director has some otherworldly friends.

Your best chance of seeing the ghostly

reader and his companion is during the daytime. And while you're in the library, be sure to visit the teen room because it is considered to be the most haunted part of the building. Library patrons and staff often get an uneasy feeling in the area. Witnesses report hearing books shifting around on the shelves when no one is nearby. Because of the odd phenomena, employees avoid working in the teen room alone.

One Halloween, the library invited paranormal investigators to explore the library after closing time. The experts found themselves strangely drawn to the teen room.

Participants gathered there in a circle, and immediately, the hair stood up on the backs of their necks and many broke out in goosebumps. But Shetter wasn't afraid—she thinks the ghosts who live in the library are friendly: "It felt like a rush of puppies coming up to greet me. It was like whatever was there that night was happy to see me."

After you've explored the library, travel ten miles down the road to the Belen Harvey House Museum, where many people have reported uncanny happenings.

In 1910, the Atchison, Topeka & Santa Fe Railway reached the town of Belen and made it the "Hub City" for New Mexico, serving all trains traveling north-south and east-west. And because Belen became a busy crossroads for travelers and freight, it also gained a Harvey House.

Fred Harvey established Harvey Houses along western railroad routes. Harvey Houses were restaurants and hotels for train passengers back in the days when such hospitality was scarce. Some say Fred Harvey invented "fast food" because diners had only thirty minutes to eat before they reboarded their train and continued their journey. Harvey Houses were known for good food and excellent service provided by waitresses known as Harvey Girls.

The Belen Harvey House was a busy stop on the railroad route until 1940. Then, the building became a Reading Room, which was a library, entertainment center, and hostel for railroad workers. In the 1980s, the building became a community center, and finally, today, it is a museum housing the Belen Model Railroad Club and the Valencia County Historical Society.

It is also very haunted.

The director of the museum is quick to

confirm the claims of ghostly activities because she often observes lights turning themselves off and on again. Ghost hunters have documented an apparition of a Harvey Girl, dressed in the unmistakable uniform consisting of a black, long-sleeved dress, pristine white apron, and enormous starched white bow on the top of her head.

But that's not all. One night, an employee found himself eavesdropping on a spirited conversation. It was Christmastime, and he was decorating a display of trees at the Harvey

House after hours, when he heard two women laughing and talking downstairs. He assumed that other employees had also decided to stop by and do some late-night tasks, so he carried on with his work. When he heard the voices again, he decided he'd better let himself be known so the women wouldn't be startled by his presence.

But when he got downstairs, no one was there. He searched the first floor and found all the doors locked and all the lights off. He was the only one in the museum. Was it the ghosts of two Harvey Girls, sharing a bit of gossip during a break? Or was it a pair of phantom passengers grabbing a quick lunch as they traveled on the Atchison, Topeka & Santa Fe Railway?

Another time, the same employee was upstairs working after hours. He was standing in a hallway, looking at the light that was shining out of a room, when a human figure crossed the light and cast a shadow.

He was stunned. No one else should have been in the building, so he nervously crept down the hallway to investigate the room, the hair on his arms standing straight up. When he got to the doorway, he could tell immediately that no one was there.

The employee checked the upstairs rooms—all empty. The windows were completely blocked with Styrofoam, so the shadow could not have come from outside.

What was this baffling shadow? Was it a hungry traveler, looking for a good meal? Or a railroad worker, looking for a break from riding the rails?

These stories and others have proven that the upstairs is a hot spot for paranormal activity, and many ghost hunts have been conducted there. But if you're interested in ghosts and haunts, the Harvey House basement is another place to look. One investigator had a particularly unsettling experience in the boiler room.

The man was exploring the basement, which has a stone floor, and its dark corners are filled with strange odds and ends. The spooky atmosphere immediately set his nerves on edge. He turned on his thermal imaging camera, which is a device that registers heat to show you things you can't see with your eyes, especially in the dark.

In a gloomy corner in the boiler room, he saw a strange haze that slowly took shape as a man dressed in old-fashioned clothes. What impressed the investigator the most was the despair he saw in the apparition's eyes. Full of sympathy, he called out to the ghost, but it disappeared. Later, the witness wrote, "It appeared to me that he was looking for something, although I have no idea what it is."

Could the spirit be looking for a good meal? A place to spend the night? Or was he looking for the next train to catch? If you happen to run into the spirit as you navigate the haunted Harvey House Museum basement, perhaps he will tell you.

Dancing with a Ghost

Continue down the old Camino Real de Tierra Adentro to the city of Socorro, located about an hour south of Albuquerque. When Don Juan de Oñate brought the first Spanish settlers in 1598, they had to cross an unforgiving desert called the Jornada del Muerto, which means "Dead Man's Journey." After five thirsty days in the desert, they came across a pueblo inhabited by the Piro people, who gave them food and water. Oñate called the pueblo Socorro, which means "help" or "assistance." After that, missionaries, miners, and settlers came, but during the Pueblo Revolt of 1680, the area was abandoned and was not resettled until the early 1800s.

Mining and the arrival of the railroad made Socorro grow again, and in 1919, a luxury hotel, the Val Verde, opened its doors. By 2001, the rooms on the second floor of the hotel had been converted into apartments. And one man found he was not the *only* occupant in his unit.

One evening, when he came home from work, he noticed that all his dresser drawers and cabinet doors were standing wide open. For a moment, he felt confused. Hadn't he closed them all when he'd left that morning? The man shrugged, closed the drawers and doors, and thought nothing more of it.

The next morning before he left, he made a quick check. Yes, everything was closed and secure. But when the man came home that evening, he was stunned to find that once again, all the drawers and cabinets were open. What was going on? No one else had access to his room—he was sure of it.

He asked a ghost hunter to investigate. The ghost hunter was able to solve the mystery: Sadly, some years before, when the Val Verde was a fully functioning hotel, a man had taken his life in the room. And it seemed he was still there.

But that's not the only ghost at the Val Verde; the hotel and restaurant seem to be full of spirited visitors. Many employees have reported unsettling experiences. Bartenders have heard loud thumps coming from under the wood floor. They believe that the noise is caused by phantom hotel workers said to have died in a fire in the basement many years ago and that they are banging on the ceiling with their shovels, frantically trying to escape.

One waitress found herself in a lonely corner of the hotel restaurant all by herself. Suddenly, she heard a disembodied voice say, "How are you, my darling?" The poor waitress was so frightened, she started crying.

She no longer works there.

Another fellow was retrieving supplies from the basement when he had the eerie feeling that he was being followed. A waitress claims that she was unnerved when she saw a pitcher fly off the ice freezer and smash into a glass that was several feet away. A manager saw a "weird light" in the steakhouse and got zapped by static electricity. Reports have also been made of two ghosts who appear at the bar—a woman in a blue dress and a man in a white shirt. Who they are and what they want, no one knows.

Though many people have been scared by strange experiences in the hotel, another witness believes there's nothing to be afraid of. She said, "It's a weird feeling you get. It's not scary, but you can actually feel their [the ghosts'] presence. It doesn't make you uncomfortable."

Probably the most astounding incident happened late one night, long after the restaurant had closed. A delivery truck came after hours, and the chef and his assistant had to make many trips up and down the basement stairs, carrying boxes of the newly delivered supplies.

When all the goods were finally put away, the chef looked around for his assistant so they could leave together and he could lock up. But the assistant was nowhere to be found. So, the chef peered down the dark, narrow stairs into the basement to see whether the assistant was down there. He saw an "older man in a suit and half-shaven" staring up at him.

The chef thought his assistant was playing a trick on him and yelled, "What are you doing here?"

He was dumbfounded to hear his assistant answer him from the kitchen.

When the assistant saw his boss standing at the basement stairs with a confused expression, he came over to see what was going on. He too saw the out-of-place old man, staring up at them from the dark depths of the basement. Startled, he turned to look at the chef. And then they both looked down the stairs again. The phantom was gone.

Spooked, the pair fled without even turning off the lights.

After that, the grizzled old man appeared off and on over the years, sometimes in the basement and at other times in the dining room or the men's restroom. Some believe it is the original owner of the Val Verde Hotel. Others believe it may be one of the many people who took their lives in the hotel over the years.

The residents of Socorro have many bizarre tales to tell, including the story of an unexplainable evening when the young people in town were enjoying a dance with lively music and fun. One boy spotted a hauntingly beautiful, pale girl in a white gown who he had never seen before. He asked her to dance, and they danced together all night long.

The boy thought the girl was gorgeous but a bit odd. She was stiff and cold to the touch, and she never spoke unless she was asked a question.

When the dance was over, the boy escorted her home, holding hands. Her skin was freezing cold, so he lent her his jacket. When they neared a tiny house beside the graveyard, the girl said, "This is where I live."

Then she disappeared.

The boy froze, horrified. Who was this girl? Where did she go? Her words echoed in his head: "This is where I live." Was her home that tiny house? Or was her home . . .

. . . the graveyard?

Had he been dancing with a ghost all night? The boy ran all the way home, his skin crawling.

The next morning, in the light of day, the boy had second thoughts. He had to be mistaken. No ghost would come to a dance, walk home hand in hand with a boy, and then take his jacket. He decided he must have met a strange but beautiful girl who lives in a tiny house beside the graveyard—that's all. He set out to visit the house and ask for his jacket back.

When he got there, he gathered his courage and knocked on the door. A gray-haired woman answered wearing a black shawl around her shoulders.

"I've come for my jacket," he said.

The woman frowned. "What jacket? Who are you?"

"Your daughter has it," he said. "She borrowed it last night."

The woman's eyes narrowed, and she said, angrily, "What kind of cruel prank is this? My daughter has been dead for five years."

"But—but—I saw her," stammered the boy. "Last night. I danced with her."

"Then go visit her grave," the woman growled. "Maybe you'll find your jacket there." And she slammed the door.

The boy didn't know what to do—had he danced with a ghost after all? Shaken, he asked his friends what they saw that night, but no one could quite remember the girl. They'd all been busy having fun.

News of the strange dance partner got around town. Some people believed the boy's story. Others thought he was crazy. Finally, to settle the matter, the town dug up the girl's grave and opened the casket.

There, they found the girl's body, wearing the same dress as she did at the dance . . .

. . . and where do you suppose they found the jacket?

If *you* decide to attend a dance in Socorro, be careful about who you dance with. And whatever you do, keep your jacket on.

Unrestful Nights at the Shaffer Hotel

About an hour south of Albuquerque, you'll find the town of Mountainair, "The Pinto Bean Capital of the World." It's here that Clem "Pop" Shaffer built the Shaffer Hotel in 1923 and added a restaurant a few years later. Today, you can stop by for a hearty lunch and admire the ceiling Pop painted with Native motifs.

You may be startled to see a symbol throughout the building that has come to represent evil: the swastika. The German Nazis stole the symbol of the swastika to represent themselves, but long before there were Nazis, many ancient cultures across the world, including Native Americans, used the swastika as a symbol of healing and good luck.

The hotel and restaurant certainly enjoyed good luck for decades, serving railroad passengers and cowboys. Though it fell into disrepair for a while, the buildings are open again and ready for business. And some say, Pop is still right there to greet visitors.

Many employees attest that the "cowboy rooms" are paranormal hotspots. The cowboy rooms are small guest rooms that only contain a single bed; these rooms share a communal bathroom. It is said that these rooms served cowboys during the 1900s. Often, hotel employees hear strange noises, banging, and footsteps coming from the cowboy rooms when they are unoccupied.

When the disturbances first started happening, the workers thought people might be breaking into the building to make trouble. So, the hotel changed the locks on the doors to make sure no one could enter the rooms without a key. Everyone was surprised when the commotion continued, and it still continues to this day. Sometimes, when employees investigate, they find small footprints in the freshly vacuumed rugs. The workers assume they were left by a ghost child who once lived in the hotel.

One employee got some good advice from an unseen helper. She was cleaning the wedding suite, which is the largest room in the hotel and has a freestanding, claw-foot tub. She was standing in the tub, cleaning the windows, and couldn't quite reach the top of the glass. She decided to climb up on the edge of the tub so she could reach the entire window, when she heard a voice shout, "Don't do it!"

Startled, she whipped around—but no one was there. The door to the wedding suite was closed, and she was totally alone. All of a sudden, a disturbing image flashed into her mind. She saw herself standing on the edge of the tub, losing her footing, and falling against the glass and out the second-floor window. Unnerved, she found another way to clean the windows, thankful for the warning from a helpful spirit.

Who was it that saved the housekeeper from a terrible accident? We can't be sure, but witnesses often report sitting on the bed in the wedding suite and looking in the mirror that hangs on the wardrobe cupboard, only to see a woman standing behind them. When they turn to shoo the intruder out of the room, they are chilled to find that no one is there. The employees can confirm that the description of the ghostly woman perfectly resembles Mrs. Shaffer, Pop's wife.

Ever wonder what happens when you tease a ghost? Take a lesson from one man who found out the hard way not to taunt the spirit world.

Rooms 17 and 18 are known as the Jack and Jill rooms; they are connected by a shared bathroom. Unfortunately, the rooms have a sad past. In 1928, a cowboy was in town by himself to attend an auction. For reasons that nobody knows, the cowboy hanged himself in the bathroom.

Pop Shaffer tried to identify the man so he could notify the next of kin, but when he checked the hotel register, he found that no one had signed in. He inquired around town, but no one knew the cowboy. Finally, Pop buried the nameless cowboy in the public cemetery.

Within a few years, strange phenomena began to happen in the Jack and Jill rooms.

First, a visiting family had a spooky encounter. When they checked into the hotel, they were warned about the eerie reputation of rooms 17 and 18, but the father didn't believe in such nonsense. He mocked the cowboy ghost. "Show yourself!" he challenged. Later that evening, the man retired to room 18, and the children bedded down in room 17.

In the middle of the night, the man woke up to use the bathroom where the cowboy had ended his life. Before he could attend to his business, the father found himself slammed against the bathroom wall, pinned by an unseen energy.

Terrified, he hollered for his kids to help him. They sprang out of bed and ran to the bathroom door, but they couldn't open it. The door was stuck, and no matter how they pushed and pulled, it wouldn't budge.

The man struggled and thrashed, desperate to get away. He strained against his invisible

attacker as his children yelled and banged against the door until finally, when they had nearly given up, the enraged ghost let go of the man. As he slumped to the floor, the door popped open. The children burst in and lifted their father to his feet.

They wanted to leave the hotel—now! The father agreed. The family threw their clothes in their suitcases and yanked on the door to the hall—

—but it was locked! They ran through the bathroom and tried the door in room 17—it was also locked! The family beat on the doors and jangled the locks. They begged the ghost to let them go, apologizing for making fun of him. Finally, at 4:00 a.m., the door swung open, and the family tumbled into the hall and down the stairs. They checked out in a hurry, the father vowing to never, ever mock a ghost again.

Another family stayed in the room and had a similar but less violent story. The father, who stayed in room 18, woke up in the middle of the night to use the bathroom. Suddenly, he felt a chill. He turned to see the outline of a body on his bed.

Spooked, he rushed through the connecting bathroom and tried to open the door to his children's room—but it was locked. He yelled and beat on the door until his children woke up—but they couldn't open the door either.

Somehow, the family must have talked the ghost into letting them go because the next morning, the desk clerk came into work and found the man and his crying children waiting to check out. Which they did, without waiting for a refund.

Pop, the original owner, was also an expert furniture builder, but some of his handiwork became such a nuisance, the latest hotel owners had to put it in storage.

One day, a family rented the room that had Pop's handmade rocking chair in it. They placed one of their suitcases on the rocking chair so they could unpack. But when they opened their suitcase—*Wham!* Suddenly, it slammed itself closed, and odd creaks and groans echoed through the room.

Surprisingly, the family took the haunting in stride and managed to stay in the room throughout the night. Could you be that brave?

It wasn't the first or the last time the rocking chair caused mischief. As complaints came in, the hotel moved the chair from one room to another, until finally, employees had enough. They put the rocking chair into storage.

Would you stay in a hotel where a chair rocks by itself, phantom footprints appear in the carpet, or ghosts lock you in your room? If so, the Shaffer Hotel and Restaurant is the place for you. And if you're ready for more phantoms, turn the page to take a road trip down Interstate 25 near the Rio Salado.

The Frantic Ghost of the Rio Salado

Who is haunting the Rio Salado near Interstate 25?

Sightings of a ghoulish woman have been reported in the area since at least 1940, though the ghost's identity is up for debate. Some say it is a real-life murder victim, and others say it is the legendary La Llorona. Whoever it is, keep your doors locked when you find yourself near the rest area at mile marker 166.

La Llorona is Spanish for "wailing woman," which describes this well-known ghost perfectly. La Llorona was once a beautiful lady who met a handsome soldier and fell in love. They had two children together.

One day, La Llorona was washing clothes in the river as her two children played in the water. Her heart was broken because she had heard a rumor that the soldier she loved was going to marry someone richer and more important than she was.

A torrential rain began in the nearby mountains, and the water rushed down into the river. Suddenly, the calm water became a raging flood, and La Llorona's two children were swept away. As the children screamed, she jumped into the river to the save them, but tragically, she could not. La Llorona and her children drowned.

People have spotted La Llorona all over the Southwest, but many believe she appears most frequently near the Rio Salado. One couple insists they spotted her in the gully near the Interstate 25 rest stop. Late one night, while driving home from Albuquerque, they noticed a faint figure in the distance. As they got nearer, they saw a woman wearing a long gray dress, wringing her hands as she frantically searched the area.

The couple slowed. What was a lone woman doing wandering the desert in the middle of the night? As their car crept closer and closer, chills ran up their spines. This was no ordinary woman. She was otherworldly, ragged, and wild-looking. Terrified, the driver stepped on the gas, and the couple drove away as fast as they could.

They were convinced they had encountered the withered ghost of La Llorona, and they knew better than to fall into her trap. And if you find yourself on Interstate 25 late at night and hear La Llorona's desperate pleas for her children's safety, run—for as the legend says, she may steal you away.

The ghost of the Rio Salado may be La Llorona, or it may be a woman who was murdered in 1937. Rose Garcia became romantically involved with the man she worked for, but she soon grew tired of him. The man wanted to marry Rose, and when she refused, he murdered her and buried her in the desert. Within three years, the haunting began.

The first person to spot Rose's ghost was a truck driver who was traveling through the area on old Highway 85, which was the route through the area before Interstate 25 was built. Early in the morning, before sunrise, he passed near the Rio Salado, where he saw a young woman walking.

Surprised to see a woman wandering by herself in the middle of the desert, he slowed, rolled down his window, and asked her if she needed help. Cryptically, she shouted at him, "It wasn't me! Take me home! I want to go back!"

As the man tried to make sense of what the strange woman was saying, he was astonished to see her slowly fade away, until he was left alone in the dark.

The stunned truck driver sped down the road to the first place he found open, the Coronado Café in Socorro. He told his hair-raising story to anyone who would listen.

Over the years, many witnesses have reported seeing a barefoot woman walking along the highway, down the gully, or near the Rio Salado. Most say she cries out into the night, looking for something—or someone. But no one knows what or who.

Perhaps the most unnerving testimony comes from a police officer who had a strange experience in the same vicinity. Police officers are trained to be excellent observers. Their jobs depend on it. And their reputations. So, when a police officer attests to having a paranormal experience, researchers pay close attention.

The police officer stated that something weird happened to him when he worked at the Acacia weigh station a mile south of the rest area. One inky-black night, his shift was over and he was preparing to leave when he heard the hysterical cries of a woman shouting for help somewhere in the distance.

The officer jumped over a barbed wire fence and followed the cries. He trotted for fifty feet until he came upon old Highway 85, where the woman's cries became louder. He continued on foot down the old highway for three-quarters of a mile until he came upon a sandy ditch near the Rio Salado.

There, he saw the dark silhouette of a woman. She stood in the ditch, her hair blowing wildly in the wind and her gauzy dress dancing around her; she was frantically waving her arms. The officer raised his flashlight and shined it on the figure and—

—it promptly *vanished.*

For a moment the police officer froze. He knew what he'd just seen: a woman, solid and real. He raced to the spot where he'd plainly seen her standing and searched frantically. But no one was there.

Spooked, the officer returned to his car, unable to explain who he saw or what happened to her.

"I've been back to the weigh station since then," he explained. "But I have never encountered something like that again. It's on the wildlife refuge, so it is closed to the public and out in the middle of nowhere. If it was a woman, I have no idea how she would have evaded me."

Ghosts are like that. They are here, and then they are gone. Seemingly solid, and then transparent. A squeeze on the shoulder, and then . . . a breath on the wind.

Too many people have seen the ghost of Rio Salado to deny her existence. Is it La Llorona, searching for her children? Rose Garcia, searching for justice? Or does some other spirit haunt the area? Answers are hard to come by when you're ghost hunting, as you will see when you turn the page.

Strange Specters in Albuquerque

End your ghost hunt in historic Albuquerque, which was established by Spanish colonists in 1706. The more than three-hundred-year-old town square, Old Town Plaza, is still a bustling area of town today.

If you want to spot a ghost in broad daylight, find the alley near the hat shop on San Felipe Street. In the old days, this alley led to a row of saloons and hospitality houses. And it seems that one of the long-dead workers is still hanging around.

This Old Town Plaza ghost has been spotted so many times, she has a name: Scarlett. Employees at nearby restaurants have reported seeing the lost spirit since the 1990s.

Witnesses who work in nearby restaurants describe seeing Scarlett suddenly appear in their storage rooms among the produce and the spices. As she moves past the shelves, she rearranges things to her own liking. And when workers try to stop her, she simply disappears.

There's a good chance that you, too, may see Scarlett. She often shows up during the day in a blue or purple dress, her red hair flaming in the southwestern sun. Stop in at lunchtime on the plaza because that seems to be her favorite time of day to materialize.

Often, her lonely figure is spotted at the end of the alley that once led to this district. Newer employees and visitors frequently mistake Scarlett for a living unhoused person. Some have even called social services, but Scarlett is beyond the agency's help.

A sympathetic waitress was determined to feed the forlorn woman, so she brought her a plate of food from the restaurant. But as the waitress approached, Scarlett retreated farther and farther down the alley, until finally, she vanished.

One visitor to the area is sure he encountered Scarlett. He and his girlfriend had just finished lunch, and he waited outside the Old Town Emporium as his girlfriend went inside. He wanted to smoke a cigarette, but his lighter wouldn't work.

Just then, he spied a woman in the alley, leaning against the wall, wearing a purple dress tied at the waist; her red hair was piled on top of her head. She was smoking a cigarette. The man approached the woman to ask for a light, but as he got closer, his girlfriend called out to him. He spun around to answer and then turned back to the mysterious woman—

—but she was gone without a trace.

The man was startled; no ordinary woman could have disappeared so quickly. Had he seen a ghost?

One couple may have come across definitive proof of the Scarlett haunting. On a snowy day, they were leaving Old Town Plaza after a hearty lunch when they heard sobbing. They investigated and saw a woman at the end of the alley, pacing back and forth—a redhead in a purple dress.

They continued to their car and then thought better of it, so they turned back to see if they could help the woman. But when they got to the alley, it was empty. All that was left were some high-heeled footprints in the fresh snow where they had seen the woman pacing. But there were no footprints leading into the alley. Or out.

How did the woman get into the alley? And how did she leave? Did she just appear out of thin air and then vanish?

In 1880, the railroad arrived, and the sleepy town of Albuquerque began to grow. Suddenly, the new downtown area was flooded with travelers, cowboys, merchants, miners, and railroad workers. More than one hundred saloons popped up along Central Avenue and its side streets.

This section of town was wild and full of drinkers, gamblers, and other rough customers. Things were so bad, the district acquired a nickname: Hell's Half Acre.

When you tour downtown, look for a ghost that has been around since the 1890s: Alcaria Baca. She was found murdered in her small room between Third and Fourth Streets. Her murder was never solved.

But just a few years after her death, strange stories circulated. Witnesses reported seeing a figure dressed in a light pink nightgown popping out of the shadows in alleyways in the early morning hours. Others said they heard heart-stopping whispers coming from the darkness, a door slamming, and then the unmistakable aroma of strong perfume. Still others saw shadows, felt as though they were being watched, and heard footsteps from an unseen person stomping down the alley.

These eyewitness reports have continued from the 1890s until today. Not too long ago, a woman and her husband were walking back to their room at the Clyde hotel. She smelled an overpowering perfume and followed the scent into an alley. As she turned into the alley, a breathy female voice whispered in her ear,

"Don't trust him." The woman broke out in goosebumps as a feeling of doom came over her. Was it Alcaria, warning her to be careful, lest she too meet her demise in Hell's Half Acre?

Even people riding in cars as they pass through the area are not safe from the phantom. Several eyewitnesses have spoken about a dark figure who suddenly emerges from the shadows and darts in front of the moving cars. Drivers slam on their brakes, their tires squealing, only to find the street empty. Is it Alcaria, fleeing her murderer?

A few miles north of Hell's Half Acre, off Sawmill Road, you will find the Painted Lady, another saloon founded in the 1880s. The Painted Lady started out as the Swastika Saloon, serving lumber mill workers, miners, and cowboys. The current owner, Jesse Herron, rehabilitated the property with its bloodstained floors into a brewery and boutique hotel.

Well known for wild brawls and shootouts, the Painted Lady has a different reputation today: haunted. Herron has firsthand knowledge of the strange happenings at the brewery because odd things started occurring the moment he arrived.

The ghosts were clumsy, Herron claims. They moved things around. They bumped into things. They rattled and clomped and made all kinds of noise. At first, the odd noises and strange shadows were amusing, but over time, Herron's amusement turned to anxiety.

Herron called on a psychic, who is a person believed to sense spirits and supernatural things that others cannot. The psychic told Herron that a ghost crawled into bed with him at night. He was astonished that the psychic knew that he had a nightly visitor. He had felt the bed jiggle and vibrate many times, as if something unseen would lie down in bed next to him. He'd also seen an apparition floating above his head as he fell asleep, and sometimes, he saw her standing by his bedside. She looked to be about twelve and Hispanic, her hair pulled tightly in a bun.

Perhaps the most frightening room on the property is one of the hotel rooms called the Herron Suite. As the story goes, in this room, a man confronted his girlfriend, who was with another man, and killed them both with an axe. Then, he shot himself in the head.

Herron had a lot of trouble with the resulting haunting. His dog refused to enter the Herron Suite. And Herron couldn't blame him—he too could feel dark energy engulf him when he crossed the threshold. So, in 2014, Herron called in a Buddhist priestess to clear the area of evil and send the lingering spirits to the other side.

Today, only friendly spirits remain. Friendly or not, are you brave enough to pay them a visit?

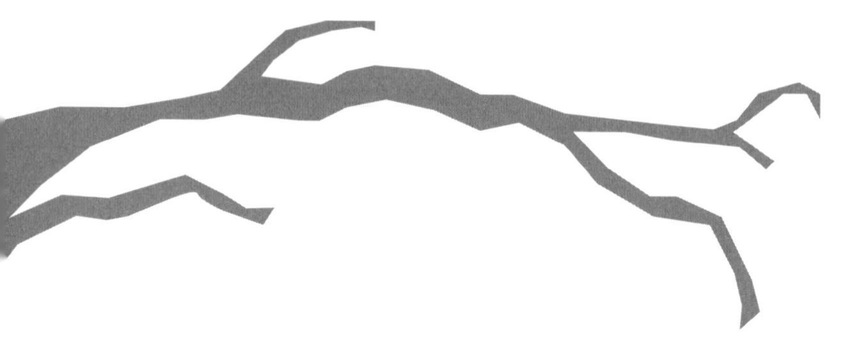

A Ghostly Goodbye

Central New Mexico is a hauntingly beautiful area with a rich culture, fascinating history, and friendly people. But some visitors—like you—know that Central New Mexico has a hidden story to tell. Will you listen?

While you admire the old buildings and enjoy the stark scenery, take the time to peek around corners and investigate the shadows. Maybe you'll spot the ghost of a miner, relaxing after a hard day underground. Or run into the spirit of a Harvey girl, bustling between the kitchen and her tables. You might even meet a long-dead mistress of a mansion, who will offer to read you a book.

Many paranormal investigators and other people have witnessed strange things in Central New Mexico, but the skeptics are hard to convince. In the end, each of us has to consider the facts and decide—are ghosts real?

What do you believe?

LISHA CAUTHEN has investigated the haunted alleys of Old Town Plaza and walked the spooky streets of Madrid. She currently writes in the attic of a one-hundred-year-old house built on a Civil War battlefield in Kansas City, Missouri, inspired by phantom footsteps and ghostly whispers. This is her seventh book of Ghostly Tales in the *Spooky America* series.

Check out some of the other *Spooky America* titles available now!

Spooky America was adapted from the creeptastic *Haunted America* series for adults. *Haunted America* explores historical haunts in cities and regions across America. Here's more from the original *Ghost Stories of Central New Mexico* author, Cody Polston.

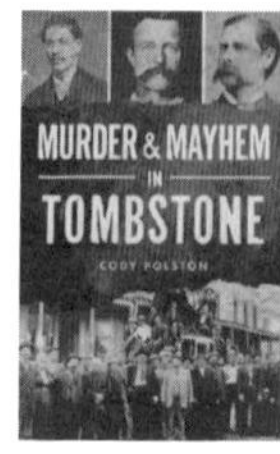